THIS BOOK

BELONGS TO

....

....

Author's Afterthoughts

With so many books out there to choose from, I want to thank you for choosing this one and taking precious time out of your life to buy and read my work. Readers like you are the reason I take such passion in creating these books.

It is with gratitude and humility that I express how honored I am to become a part of your life and I hope that you take the same pleasure in reading this book as I did in writing it.

Can I ask one small favour? I ask that you write an honest and open review on Amazon of what you thought of the book. This will help other readers make an informed choice on whether to buy this book.

My sincerest thanks.

Copyright @2023

All rights reserved. No part of this publication may be reproduced, stored in a retrieval system, or transmitted in any form or by any means, electronic, mechanical, photocopying, recording or otherwise, without the prior written permission of the Publisher.

Table Of Contents

Delicious One-Pot Meals to Please Everyone   27

Mediterranean Chicken Soup

Moroccan Chicken and Butternut Squash Soup

Chicken and Ricotta Meatball Soup

Bean, Chicken and Sausage Soup

Slow Cooker Chicken Broccoli Soup

Lentil and Ground Beef Soup

Italian Meatball Soup

Fish and Noodle Soup

Lentil, Barley and Kale Soup

Spinach and Mushroom Soup

Broccoli and Potato Soup

Moroccan Lentil Soup

Beetroot and Carrot Soup

Celery, Apple and Carrot Soup

Pumpkin and Bell Pepper Soup

Creamy Potato Soup

Wild Mushroom Soup

Spinach, Leek and Quinoa Soup

Vegetable Quinoa Soup

Slow Cooker Tuscan-style Soup

Lamb and Potato Casserole

Mediterranean Baked Fish   30

Mediterranean Chicken Casserole

Chicken and Potato Casserole

Mediterranean Chicken Drumstick Casserole

Greek Chicken Casserole

Chicken with Almonds and Prunes

Chicken and Rice Casserole

Easy Chicken Paella

Chicken and Artichoke Rice

Easy Chicken Parmigiana

One-Pot Chicken Dijonnaise

Sweet and Sour Sicilian Chicken

Lemon Rosemary Chicken

Chicken and Bacon Frittata

Chicken and Zucchini Frittata

Beef and Pumpkin Stew

Beef and Onion Stew

Beef Stew with Green Peas

Beef and Spinach Stew

Mediterranean Beef Casserole

Beef and Broccoli Stir Fry

Beef Stew with Quince

Spanish Beef Stew

Ground Beef and Chickpea Casserole

Spinach with Ground Beef

Delicious One-Pot Ground Beef Pasta

Sausage and Beans

Mediterranean Pork Casserole

Pork and Rice Casserole

Pork Roast with Cabbage

Orange Pork Chops

Pork and Mushroom Crock Pot

Bacon and Mushroom Frittata

Brussels Sprouts with Bacon and Onion

Zucchini Bake

Baked Cauliflower

Potato and Zucchini Bake

Artichoke and Onion Frittata

Green Pea and Mushroom Stew

Tomato and Leek Stew

Potato and Leek Stew

Baked Beans and Rice Casserole

Creamy Green Pea and Rice Casserole

Zucchini and Rice Stew

Spinach with Rice

Eggplant Casserole

Eggplant and Chickpea Casserole

Ratatouille

Rice Stuffed Bell Peppers

Green Bean and Potato Stew

Cabbage and Rice Stew

Rice with Leeks and Olives

Rice and Tomato Stew

Okra and Tomato Casserole

Spinach with Eggs

Mish-Mash

Vegetable Quinoa Pilaf

Spinach, Lentil and Quinoa Casserole

Rich Vegetable One-Pot Pasta

One-Pot Broccoli Pasta

FREE BONUS RECIPES: 10 Ridiculously Easy Jam and Jelly Recipes Anyone Can Make

SUMMARY

The Allure of One-Pot Meals:

One-pot meals have gained immense popularity in recent years due to their convenience, simplicity, and delicious flavors. These meals, as the name suggests, are prepared using just one pot or pan, making the cooking process much easier and hassle-free. From soups and stews to pasta dishes and casseroles, the possibilities for one-pot meals are endless.

One of the main reasons why one-pot meals have become so alluring is their convenience. With our busy lifestyles, finding time to cook elaborate meals can be a challenge. One-pot meals offer a solution by allowing us to prepare a complete and satisfying meal in a single pot. This means less time spent on preparation and cleanup, making it a perfect option for those who are short on time or simply prefer to spend less time in the kitchen.

In addition to their convenience, one-pot meals also offer a great way to experiment with flavors and ingredients. By cooking everything together in one pot, the flavors have a chance to meld and develop, resulting in a dish that is rich and flavorful. Whether you're using fresh vegetables, aromatic herbs, or a combination of spices, one-pot meals allow you to create complex and delicious flavors with minimal effort.

Furthermore, one-pot meals are incredibly versatile. You can easily adapt them to suit your dietary preferences or accommodate any dietary restrictions. Whether you're a vegetarian, vegan, or follow a gluten-free or dairy-free diet, there are countless one-pot meal recipes available that cater to your specific needs. This versatility makes one-pot meals a great option for families or groups with different dietary requirements, as everyone can enjoy a delicious and satisfying meal together.

Another advantage of one-pot meals is their ability to save money. By using just one pot or pan, you can minimize the number of kitchen tools and utensils needed, reducing the cost of your meal preparation. Additionally, one-pot meals often utilize affordable ingredients such as grains, legumes, and seasonal vegetables, making them a budget-friendly option for those looking to save money on groceries.

Lastly, one-pot meals are not only delicious and convenient, but they also offer a healthier alternative to many traditional cooking methods. By cooking everything together, you can retain more nutrients in your food compared to methods like boiling or frying. Additionally, one-pot meals often require less oil or fat, making them a healthier option for those looking to reduce their calorie intake or maintain a balanced diet.

Benefits of One-Pot Cooking:

One-pot cooking refers to the method of preparing a meal using only one cooking vessel, such as a pot or a pan. This cooking technique has gained popularity in recent years due to its numerous benefits.

One of the main advantages of one-pot cooking is its convenience. With this method, you can save time and effort by reducing the number of dishes and utensils used in the cooking process. Instead of juggling multiple pots and pans, you can simply throw all the ingredients into one pot and let them cook together. This not only simplifies the cooking process but also makes cleanup much easier.

Another benefit of one-pot cooking is its versatility. You can prepare a wide variety of dishes using this method, from soups and stews to pasta and stir-fries. The possibilities are endless, allowing you to experiment with different flavors and ingredients. Additionally, one-pot cooking is a great way to use up leftover ingredients, as you can easily incorporate them into a single dish.

One-pot cooking is also known for its ability to enhance the flavors of the ingredients. When all the ingredients are cooked together in one pot, their flavors meld together, creating a rich and complex taste. This is especially true for dishes that require simmering or slow cooking, as the flavors have more time to develop and intensify. The result is a delicious and satisfying meal that is bursting with flavor.

Furthermore, one-pot cooking is a cost-effective option. By using only one cooking vessel, you can save money on buying multiple pots and pans. Additionally, this method allows you to make the most of cheaper cuts of meat or vegetables, as the slow cooking process helps tenderize them and bring out their natural flavors. This means you can create delicious and nutritious meals without breaking the bank.

One-pot cooking is also a great option for those with limited kitchen space. If you have a small kitchen or lack storage space, having fewer pots and pans can be a game-changer. With one-pot cooking, you can still enjoy a variety of meals without cluttering your kitchen with unnecessary cookware.

Lastly, one-pot cooking is a healthier option compared to other cooking methods. Since the ingredients are cooked together, there is minimal need for added fats or oils. This can help reduce the overall calorie and fat content of the dish, making it a healthier choice. Additionally, one-pot cooking often involves using fresh and whole ingredients, which are packed with essential nutrients and vitamins.

Overview of Cooking Methods Covered: Throughout the course, we will cover a variety of cooking methods that are essential for any aspiring chef to master. These methods include sautéing, roasting, grilling, braising, poaching, and baking.

Sautéing is a quick and easy method that involves cooking food in a small amount of oil or butter over high heat. This method is perfect for cooking vegetables, meats, and seafood, and can be used to create a variety of dishes such as stir-fries, omelets, and pan-seared steaks.

Roasting is a dry heat cooking method that involves cooking food in an oven at a high temperature. This method is perfect for cooking large cuts of meat, poultry, and vegetables, and can be used to create dishes such as roasted chicken, beef tenderloin, and roasted root vegetables.

Grilling is a popular cooking method that involves cooking food over an open flame or hot coals. This method is perfect for cooking meats, seafood, and vegetables, and can be used to create dishes such as grilled steak, shrimp skewers, and grilled vegetables.

Braising is a slow-cooking method that involves cooking food in a liquid over low heat for an extended period of time. This method is perfect for cooking tough cuts of meat, and can be used to create dishes such as beef stew, pot roast, and braised short ribs.

Poaching is a gentle cooking method that involves cooking food in a liquid at a low temperature. This method is perfect for cooking delicate foods such as fish, eggs, and fruit, and can be used to create dishes such as poached salmon, eggs Benedict, and poached pears.

Baking is a dry heat cooking method that involves cooking food in an oven at a moderate temperature. This method is perfect for cooking bread, pastries, and desserts, and can be used to create dishes such as homemade bread, apple pie, and chocolate cake.

By mastering these cooking methods, you will be able to create a wide variety of delicious and impressive dishes that will impress your family and friends.

Essential Kitchen Tools and Equipment:

When it comes to setting up a functional and efficient kitchen, having the right tools and equipment is essential. Whether you're a seasoned chef or just starting out, having the right kitchen tools can make all the difference in the world. From basic utensils to specialized gadgets, here are some essential kitchen tools and equipment that every home cook should have in their arsenal.

1. Knives: A good set of knives is the cornerstone of any kitchen. A chef's knife, paring knife, and serrated knife are the three essential knives that every home cook should have. Invest in high-quality knives that are comfortable to hold and maintain a sharp edge.

2. Cutting boards: Having a few different cutting boards on hand is essential for preventing cross-contamination and keeping your knives in good condition. Look for cutting boards made of wood, plastic, or bamboo, and make sure to have separate boards for meat, poultry, and vegetables.

3. Mixing bowls: A set of mixing bowls in various sizes is essential for prepping and mixing ingredients. Look for bowls that are durable, easy to clean, and have a non-slip base to prevent them from sliding around on the countertop.

4. Measuring cups and spoons: Accurate measurements are crucial in cooking and baking, so having a set of measuring cups and spoons is a must. Look for a set that includes both dry and liquid measurements, and make sure they are made of durable materials that won't warp or break over time.

5. Pots and pans: A good set of pots and pans is essential for cooking a wide variety of dishes. Look for a mix of non-stick and stainless steel pans, as well as a few different sizes of saucepans and skillets to cover all your cooking needs.

6. Utensils: A set of basic kitchen utensils including a spatula, slotted

spoon, tongs, and whisk is essential for cooking and serving food. Look for utensils made of heat-resistant materials that won't scratch your cookware.

7. Food processor or blender: A food processor or blender is essential for making sauces, soups, smoothies, and more. Look for a model with a powerful motor and a variety of attachments to cover all your food processing needs.

8. Baking sheets and pans: If you enjoy baking, having a set of baking sheets, cake pans, and muffin tins is essential.

Basic Ingredients to Keep on Hand:

When it comes to cooking, having a well-stocked pantry is essential. It not only saves you time and money, but it also allows you to whip up delicious meals at a moment's notice. So, what are the basic ingredients that you should always keep on hand? Let's dive in and explore!

First and foremost, a variety of spices and seasonings is a must. These little powerhouses can transform a bland dish into a flavorful masterpiece. Some essential spices to have include salt, pepper, garlic powder, onion powder, paprika, cumin, and oregano. Additionally, having a selection of dried herbs like basil, thyme, and rosemary can add depth to your dishes.

Next, a range of cooking oils is essential for various cooking methods. Olive oil is a versatile option that can be used for sautéing, roasting, and dressing salads. Vegetable oil or canola oil is great for frying and baking. If you enjoy Asian cuisine, having sesame oil and soy sauce on hand can elevate your stir-fries and marinades.

Stocking up on canned goods is also a smart move. Canned tomatoes, both diced and crushed, are incredibly versatile and can be used as a base for sauces, soups, and stews. Canned beans, such as black beans, chickpeas, and kidney beans, are excellent sources of protein and can be added to salads, chili, or used to make homemade hummus.

Pasta and rice are pantry staples that can be used as a base for countless meals. Whether you prefer spaghetti, penne, or macaroni, having a variety of pasta shapes ensures you can create different dishes. Rice, on the other hand, can be used in stir-fries, pilafs, or as a side dish.

Don't forget about canned or jarred sauces and condiments. Tomato sauce, barbecue sauce, and mayonnaise are just a few examples of versatile ingredients that can be used to enhance the flavor of your dishes. Mustard, ketchup, and hot sauce are also great additions to have on hand for adding a kick to your meals.

Having a selection of canned or dried fruits and vegetables is a smart move for those times when fresh produce is not readily available. Canned corn, peas, and green beans can be added to casseroles or used as side dishes.

Tips for Preparing and Organizing:

Tips for Preparing and Organizing

Preparing and organizing are essential skills that can help you stay focused, save time, and reduce stress. Whether you are preparing for a big event, a project at work, or simply trying to stay organized in your daily life, these tips can help you streamline your tasks and achieve your goals more efficiently.

1. Make a to-do list: Start by creating a comprehensive to-do list that includes all the tasks you need to complete. This will help you visualize your workload and prioritize your tasks accordingly. Break down larger tasks into smaller, more manageable subtasks to make them less overwhelming.

2. Set deadlines: Assign deadlines to each task on your to-do list. This will create a sense of urgency and help you stay on track. Be realistic when setting deadlines and consider the time required for each task. Avoid overloading yourself with too many tasks in a short period of time.

3. Prioritize tasks: Determine which tasks are most important and need to be completed first. Consider the urgency and importance of each task and prioritize accordingly. Focus on high-priority tasks to ensure that they are completed on time and don't get overshadowed by less important tasks.

4. Create a schedule: Once you have prioritized your tasks, create a schedule that outlines when you will work on each task. Allocate specific time slots for each task and stick to the schedule as much as possible. This will help you stay organized and ensure that you allocate enough time for each task.

5. Break tasks into smaller steps: If you have a particularly complex or time-consuming task, break it down into smaller, more manageable steps. This will make the task seem less daunting and

help you make progress more easily. Celebrate each small accomplishment to stay motivated and maintain momentum.

6. Gather necessary resources: Before starting a task, gather all the necessary resources and materials you will need. This includes any documents, tools, or equipment required to complete the task. Having everything ready beforehand will save you time and prevent unnecessary interruptions.

7. Minimize distractions: Create a conducive work environment by minimizing distractions. Turn off notifications on your phone or computer, close unnecessary tabs or applications, and find a quiet space where you can focus. If you find it difficult to concentrate, consider using productivity tools or techniques such as the Pomodoro Technique.

8. Delegate tasks: If possible, delegate tasks to others to lighten your workload. Identify tasks that can be done by someone else and assign them accordingly.

Choosing the Right Skillet:

When it comes to cooking, having the right tools is essential, and one of the most important tools in any kitchen is a skillet. Skillets are versatile and can be used for a wide range of cooking techniques, from frying and sautéing to searing and baking. However, with so many options available on the market, choosing the right skillet can be a daunting task. In this guide, we will explore the factors to consider when selecting a skillet and provide you with the information you need to make an informed decision.

First and foremost, it is important to consider the material of the skillet. Skillets are commonly made from stainless steel, cast iron, non-stick coated aluminum, or copper. Each material has its own unique properties and advantages. Stainless steel skillets are durable, non-reactive, and distribute heat evenly, making them a popular choice among professional chefs. Cast iron skillets, on the other hand, are known for their excellent heat retention and even heating, making them ideal for searing and frying. Non-stick coated aluminum skillets are lightweight and easy to clean, making them a convenient option for everyday cooking. Lastly, copper skillets offer superior heat conductivity and precise temperature control, but they can be quite expensive.

Another important factor to consider is the size of the skillet. Skillets come in various sizes, ranging from 8 inches to 14 inches in diameter. The size you choose should depend on the number of people you typically cook for and the type of dishes you plan to prepare. If you often cook for a large family or enjoy making one-pot meals, a larger skillet may be more suitable. However, if you primarily cook for yourself or a small household, a smaller skillet may be more practical.

The handle of the skillet is another crucial aspect to consider. The handle should be comfortable to hold and securely attached to the skillet. It is also important to ensure that the handle stays cool during cooking to prevent burns. Many skillets come with heat-resistant handles or handles that are designed to stay cool, which can greatly enhance safety and ease of use.

Additionally, it is worth considering whether you prefer a skillet with a lid or without. Skillets with lids are versatile and can be used for a wider range of cooking techniques, such as braising and simmering. They also help to retain heat and moisture, resulting in more flavorful and tender dishes. However, skillets without lids are often

Essential Skillet Cooking Techniques: Mastering the Art of Cooking with a Skillet

Skillet cooking is a versatile and essential skill that every home cook should master. Whether you're a beginner or an experienced cook, understanding the fundamental techniques of skillet cooking can elevate your culinary creations to new heights. In this guide, we will explore the various techniques and tips that will help you become a skilled skillet cook.

1. Preheating the Skillet: Before you start cooking, it's crucial to preheat your skillet properly. This step ensures even heat distribution and prevents food from sticking to the pan. Place the skillet on medium-high heat for a few minutes until it becomes hot. You can test the heat by sprinkling a few drops of water on the surface; if they sizzle and evaporate immediately, the skillet is ready.

2. Choosing the Right Oil: Selecting the appropriate oil for skillet cooking is essential. Different oils have different smoke points, which is the temperature at which they start to break down and produce smoke. For high-heat cooking, such as searing or stir-frying, use oils with high smoke points like canola, grapeseed, or peanut oil. For lower-heat cooking, such as sautéing or simmering, olive oil or butter can be used.

3. Searing: Searing is a technique used to brown the surface of meat, fish, or vegetables quickly. It adds depth of flavor and creates a beautiful caramelized crust. To sear, heat the skillet with oil until it's hot, then add the food and let it cook undisturbed for a few minutes. Flip the food and repeat the process on the other side. Remember not to overcrowd the skillet, as it can lower the temperature and prevent proper browning.

4. Sauteing: Sauteing involves cooking food quickly in a small amount of oil or butter over medium-high heat. It's a versatile technique that can be used for a wide range of ingredients, from vegetables to proteins. To sauté, heat the skillet with oil or butter,

add the ingredients, and stir or toss them frequently to ensure even cooking. The goal is to cook the food until it's tender and lightly browned.

5. Deglazing: Deglazing is a technique used to create flavorful sauces or gravies by using the browned bits left in the skillet after cooking meat or vegetables. To deglaze, remove the cooked food

Beginner-Friendly Skillet Recipes: Beginner-Friendly Skillet Recipes are perfect for those who are just starting out in the kitchen or for those who want to try something new. Skillet recipes are easy to make and require minimal preparation time, making them ideal for busy weeknights or lazy weekends. With a few simple ingredients and a trusty skillet, you can create delicious and satisfying meals that will impress your family and friends.

One of the best things about skillet recipes is that they are versatile and can be adapted to suit your taste preferences. Whether you prefer meat, seafood, or vegetarian dishes, there is a skillet recipe out there for you. Some popular skillet recipes include chicken fajitas, shrimp scampi, and vegetable stir-fry. These recipes are not only delicious but also healthy and nutritious, making them a great choice for those who are watching their diet.

Skillet recipes are also great for those who are on a budget. With just a few ingredients, you can create a filling and satisfying meal that won't break the bank. Some budget-friendly skillet recipes include spaghetti carbonara, beef stroganoff, and chili con carne. These recipes are not only affordable but also easy to make, making them perfect for those who are short on time.

Another great thing about skillet recipes is that they are easy to clean up. Unlike other cooking methods that require multiple pots and pans, skillet recipes only require one pan, making cleanup a breeze. This is especially helpful for those who hate doing dishes or for those who have limited kitchen space.

In conclusion, Beginner-Friendly Skillet Recipes are a great way to get started in the kitchen or to try something new. With their versatility, affordability, and ease of preparation, skillet recipes are perfect for busy weeknights or lazy weekends. So why not give them a try and see what delicious meals you can create with just a trusty skillet and a few simple ingredients?

Understanding Slow Cooker Basics:

Slow cookers, also known as crock-pots, have become increasingly popular in recent years due to their convenience and ability to create delicious, flavorful meals with minimal effort. If you're new to slow cooking or looking to expand your knowledge, it's important to understand the basics of how these appliances work and how to use them effectively.

First and foremost, slow cookers are designed to cook food at a low temperature over a long period of time. This gentle cooking method allows flavors to meld together and meats to become tender and juicy. The typical temperature range for a slow cooker is between 170 and 280 degrees Fahrenheit, with most recipes calling for cooking times of 4 to 8 hours.

When using a slow cooker, it's important to choose the right size for your needs. Slow cookers come in various sizes, typically ranging from 1.5 to 8 quarts. If you're cooking for a small family or just yourself, a smaller slow cooker will suffice. However, if you're planning to cook for a crowd or want to have leftovers, a larger slow cooker may be necessary.

Before using your slow cooker, it's important to prepare your ingredients properly. This includes trimming excess fat from meats, chopping vegetables into uniform pieces, and seasoning your ingredients to taste. While slow cookers are great for one-pot meals, it's important to layer your ingredients properly to ensure even cooking. Start with the meat on the bottom, followed by any vegetables, and then add your liquid or sauce on top.

One of the benefits of slow cooking is the ability to set it and forget it. Once your ingredients are in the slow cooker, you can simply set the desired cooking time and temperature and let it do its magic. However, it's important to note that slow cookers do not reach a high enough temperature to safely cook frozen meats. Always thaw your meats before adding them to the slow cooker to avoid any potential food safety issues.

When it comes to cleaning your slow cooker, it's important to follow the manufacturer's instructions. Most slow cookers have removable stoneware inserts that can be easily cleaned with warm, soapy water. Some models are even dishwasher safe, making cleanup a breeze. It's important to avoid using abrasive cleaners or scrub brushes on the stoneware, as this can damage the non-stick coating.

In conclusion, understanding the basics of slow cooker cooking can help you create delicious, flavorful meals with minimal effort. From choosing the right
Tips for Maximizing Flavor in Slow Cooker Dishes:

Slow cookers are a fantastic tool for creating flavorful and delicious dishes with minimal effort. By taking a few extra steps and following some tips, you can maximize the flavor in your slow cooker creations and elevate them to a whole new level.

First and foremost, it's important to properly season your ingredients before adding them to the slow cooker. This means generously seasoning your meats, vegetables, and even grains with salt, pepper, and any other desired herbs and spices. This step ensures that the flavors are well-distributed throughout the dish and that every bite is bursting with taste.

Another tip for maximizing flavor is to sear your meats before adding them to the slow cooker. This step helps to develop a rich and caramelized crust on the outside of the meat, which adds depth and complexity to the overall flavor. Simply heat a skillet with some oil over high heat and sear the meat on all sides until browned. Then, transfer it to the slow cooker and continue with the recipe as usual.

In addition to searing, you can also enhance the flavor of your slow cooker dishes by sautéing your vegetables before adding them to the pot. This step helps to release their natural sugars and intensify their flavors. Heat some oil in a skillet and cook the vegetables until they are slightly softened and golden brown. Then, transfer them to the slow cooker and let them continue to cook and meld with the other ingredients.

To further enhance the flavor, consider using homemade stocks or broths instead of store-bought ones. Homemade stocks are rich in flavor and can add a depth of taste that store-bought versions often lack. You can easily make your own by simmering bones, vegetables, and aromatics in water for several hours. The resulting stock can be used as a base for your slow cooker dishes, infusing them with a homemade and robust flavor.

Another trick to maximize flavor is to layer your ingredients in the slow cooker. Start with the aromatics, such as onions, garlic, and herbs, at the bottom of the pot. These ingredients will release their flavors as they cook and infuse the entire dish. Next, add your proteins, followed by any vegetables or grains. This layering technique ensures that each ingredient has a chance to develop its own unique flavor profile while also allowing the flavors to meld together harmoniously.

Lastly, don't be afraid to experiment with different ingredients and flavor combinations. Slow cookers are incredibly versatile and can accommodate a wide range of flavors. Consider adding ingredients Simple Slow Cooker Recipes for Beginners: Simple Slow Cooker Recipes for Beginners is a comprehensive guide that aims to provide easy-to-follow recipes for individuals who are new to slow cooking. Slow cooking is a popular cooking method that allows you to prepare delicious and flavorful meals with minimal effort. This book is designed to help beginners navigate the world of slow cooking by offering a variety of simple and straightforward recipes.

The book begins with an introduction to slow cooking, explaining the benefits and advantages of this cooking method. It highlights the convenience and time-saving aspects of slow cooking, making it an ideal choice for busy individuals or those who prefer to have their meals ready when they come home from work.

The recipes in this book are carefully selected to cater to beginners who may not have much experience in the kitchen. Each recipe is accompanied by detailed instructions, including the ingredients needed, step-by-step cooking directions, and cooking times. The recipes are written in a clear and concise manner, ensuring that even those with limited cooking skills can easily follow along.

The book covers a wide range of recipes, including soups, stews, casseroles, and even desserts. It includes classic slow cooker dishes such as beef stew, chicken noodle soup, and pulled pork, as well as more unique recipes like Moroccan lamb tagine and vegetarian chili. The variety of recipes ensures that there is something for everyone, regardless of their dietary preferences or restrictions.

In addition to the recipes, the book also provides helpful tips and tricks for successful slow cooking. It offers advice on choosing the right slow cooker, understanding cooking times, and properly seasoning dishes. These tips are invaluable for beginners who may be unsure of how to get the best results from their slow cooker.

Overall, Simple Slow Cooker Recipes for Beginners is a must-have resource for anyone looking to explore the world of slow cooking. With its easy-to-follow recipes and helpful tips, this book will empower beginners to create delicious and satisfying meals with minimal effort. Whether you're a busy professional, a college student, or simply someone who wants to simplify their cooking routine, this book is the perfect companion to help you get started on your slow cooking journey.

Delicious One-Pot Meals to Please Everyone

In a world where food is full of frightening artificial additives and flavorings, there is one simple and easy way to adopt a healthier lifestyle - the more unprocessed and real food you eat, the better.

While it may look and sound difficult to cook real food at home you will soon realize you can throw together a healthy one-pot family dinner in the same amount of time you'd need to order a takeout. Homemade one-pot cooking is the easiest and stress-free way of preparing fast, yet healthy dinners for the family. When time is short and all you want is to spend more time with your family, one-pot soups, stews, casseroles and chillis are just the thing to cook. All you need to do is cut up your favorite vegetables, meats and legumes, throw them together with your favorite spices in a single pot, skillet or slow cooker and you will have a quick weeknight supper or a delicious weekend dinner - it doesn't get any easier than that!

At the end of a busy day one-pot cooking is just what you need to prepare delicious family dinners which are sure to please everyone at the table and to become all time favorites.

Mediterranean Chicken Soup

Serves 5-6

Ingredients:

1.5 lb chicken breasts

3-4 carrots, chopped

1 celery rib, chopped

1 red onion, chopped

1/3 cup rice, rinsed

8 cups water

10 black olives, pitted and halved

1/2 tsp salt

ground black pepper, to taste

lemon juice, to serve

1/2 cup fresh parsley or coriander, finely cut, to serve

Directions:

Place chicken breasts in a soup pot. Add in onion, carrots, celery, salt, pepper and water. Stir well and bring to a boil.

Add in rice and olives. Stir and reduce heat. Simmer for 30-40 minutes.

Remove chicken from the pot and let it cool. Shred it and return it back to the pot.

Serve soup with lemon juice and sprinkled with fresh parsley or coriander.

Moroccan Chicken and Butternut Squash Soup

Serves 5-6

Ingredients:

3 skinless, boneless chicken thighs (about 14 oz), cut into bite-sized pieces

1 large onion, chopped

1 zucchini, quartered lengthwise and sliced into 1/2-inch pieces

3 cups peeled butternut squash, cut in 1/2-inch pieces

2 tbsp tomato paste

4 cups chicken broth

1/3 cup uncooked couscous

3 tbsp olive oil

1/2 tsp ground cumin

1/4 tsp cinnamon

1 tsp paprika

2 tbsp fresh basil leaves, chopped

1 tbsp grated orange rind

Directions:

Heat a soup pot over medium heat. Gently sauté onion, stirring occasionally. Add in chicken pieces and cook for 3-4 minutes until chicken is brown on all sides.

Add cumin, cinnamon and paprika and stir well. Add butternut squash and tomato paste; stir again.

Add chicken broth and bring to a boil then reduce heat and simmer for ten minutes.

Stir in couscous, salt and zucchini pieces and cook until squash is tender. Remove pot from heat. Season with salt and pepper to taste. Stir in chopped basil and orange rind and serve.

Chicken and Ricotta Meatball Soup

Serves 4-5

Ingredients:

1 lb ground chicken meat

1 egg, lightly whisked

1 cup whole milk ricotta

1 cup grated Parmezan cheese

1-2 tbsp flour

1/2 onion, chopped

4 cups chicken broth

2 cups baby spinach

1/2 tsp dried oregano

3 tbsp olive oil

½ tsp black pepper

Directions:

Place ground chicken, Ricotta, Parmezan, egg and black pepper in a bowl. Combine well with hands and roll teaspoonfuls of the mixture into balls. Roll each meatball in the flour then set aside on a large plate.

In a deep soup pot, heat olive oil and gently sauté onion until transparent. Add in oregano and chicken broth and bring to a boil. Add meatballs, reduce heat, and simmer, uncovered, for 15 minutes.

Add baby spinach leaves and simmer for 2 more minutes until it wilts.

Bean, Chicken and Sausage Soup

Serves 4-5

Ingredients:

10.5 oz Italian sausage

2 bacon strips, diced

1 cup chicken, cooked and diced

1 cup canned kidney beans, rinsed and drained

1 onion, chopped

2 garlic cloves, crushed

4 cups water

1 cup canned tomatoes, diced, undrained

1 bay leaf

1 tsp dried thyme

1 tsp savory

1/2 tsp dried basil

salt and pepper, to taste

Directions:

In a deep soup pot, cook the sausage, onion and bacon over medium heat until the sausage is no longer pink. Drain off the fat. Add in the garlic and cook for a minute until just fragrant.

Add water, tomatoes and seasonings and bring to a boil. Cover, reduce heat, and simmer for 30 minutes. Add chicken and beans. Simmer for five minutes and serve.

Slow Cooker Chicken Broccoli Soup

Serves 6-7

Ingredients:

2 lb boneless chicken thighs, cut in bite sized pieces

1 small onion, chopped

1 fresh garlic clove

6-7 fresh or frozen broccoli florets

4 cups chicken broth

2 potatoes, peeled and cubed

3 tbsp olive oil

1 tsp garlic powder

1 tsp dried oregano

1 tsp salt

black pepper, to taste

12 oz cheddar cheese, to serve

Directions:

In a skillet, sauté onion and garlic with olive oil until onion is translucent.

Season the chicken well with salt, black pepper, garlic powder and oregano. Place it in slow cooker with the onion mixture and all remaining ingredients.

Cover and cook on low for 8-10 hours or on high for 4-5 hours. Serve topped with cheddar cheese.

Lentil and Ground Beef Soup

Serves 4-5

Ingredients:

1 lb ground beef

1 cup brown lentils

2 carrots, chopped

1 onion, chopped

1 potato, peeled and diced

4 garlic cloves, chopped

2 tomatoes, grated or pureed

5 cups water

1 tsp summer savory

1 tsp paprika

2 tbsp olive oil

1 tsp salt

ground black pepper, to taste

Directions:

Heat olive oil in a large soup pot. Brown the ground beef, breaking it up with a spoon. Add in paprika and garlic and stir. Add lentils, remaining vegetables, water and spice.

Bring the soup to a boil. Reduce heat to low and simmer, covered, for about an hour, or until the lentils are tender. Stir occasionally.

Italian Meatball Soup

Serves 4-5

Ingredients:

1 lb ground beef

1 small onion, grated

1 onion, chopped

2 garlic cloves, crushed

1 zucchini, diced

½ cup green beans, trimmed, halved

½ cup breadcrumbs

3-4 basil leaves, finely chopped

1/3 cup Parmesan cheese, grated

1 egg, lightly beaten

2 cups tomato sauce

3 cups water

½ cup small pasta

2 tbsp olive oil

salt and black pepper, to taste

Directions:

Combine the ground beef with grated onion, garlic, breadcrumbs, basil, Parmesan and an egg in a large bowl. Season with salt and pepper. Mix well with hands and roll tablespoonfuls of the mixture into balls. Place on a plate.

Heat olive oil into a large deep soup pot and sauté onion and garlic until transparent. Add in tomato sauce and water, and bring to a boil over high heat.

Add the meatballs, reduce heat to medium-low and simmer, uncovered, for 15 minutes. Add in pasta and cook for 5 more minutes. Add the zucchini and green beans.

Cook until pasta and vegetables are tender. Serve sprinkled with Parmesan cheese.

Fish and Noodle Soup

Serves 4-5

Ingredients:

14 oz firm white fish, cut into strips

2 carrots, cut into ribbons

1 zucchini, cut into thin ribbons

7 oz white button mushrooms, sliced

1 celery rib, finely cut

1 cup baby spinach

7 oz fresh noodles

3 cups chicken broth

2 cups water

2 tbsp soy sauce

1/2 tsp ground ginger

black pepper, to taste

Directions:

Place chicken broth, water and soy sauce in a large saucepan. Bring to a boil and add in carrots, celery, zucchini, mushrooms, ginger and noodles.

Cook, partially covered, for 3-4 minutes then add in fish and simmer for 3 minutes or until the fish is cooked through. Add baby spinach and simmer, stirring, for a minute, or until it wilts. Season with black pepper and serve.

Lentil, Barley and Kale Soup

Serves 4

Ingredients:

2 medium leeks, chopped

2 garlic cloves, chopped

2 bay leaves

1 can tomatoes, diced and undrained

1/2 cup red lentils

1/2 cup barley

1 bunch kale, coarsely chopped

4 cups vegetable broth

3 tbsp olive oil

1 tbsp paprika

½ tsp cumin

Directions:

Heat olive oil in a large saucepan over medium-high heat and sauté leeks and garlic until fragrant. Add in cumin, paprika, tomatoes, lentils, barley and vegetable broth. Season with salt and pepper.

Cover, and bring to a boil then reduce heat and simmer for 40 minutes or until barley is tender. Add in kale and let it simmer for a few minutes more until it wilts.

Spinach and Mushroom Soup

Serves 4-5

Ingredients:

1 small onion, finely cut

1 small carrot, chopped

1 small zucchini, peeled and diced

1 medium potato, peeled and diced

6-7 white button mushrooms, chopped

2 cups chopped fresh spinach

4 cups vegetable broth or water

4 tbsp olive oil

salt and black pepper, to taste

Directions:

Heat olive oil in a large soup pot over medium heat. Add in potato, onion and mushroom and cook until vegetables are soft but not mushy.

Add chopped fresh spinach, zucchini and vegetable broth and simmer for about 15 minutes. Season to taste with salt and pepper and serve.

Broccoli and Potato Soup

Serves 4-5

Ingredients:

1 lb broccoli, cut into florets

2 potatoes, peeled and chopped

1 onion, chopped

3 garlic cloves, crushed

4 cups water

2 tbsp olive oil

¼ tsp ground nutmeg

Directions:

Heat oil in a large saucepan over medium-high heat. Add in onion and garlic and sauté, stirring, for 3 minutes or until soft.

Add in broccoli, potato and 4 cups of cold water. Cover, bring to a boil, reduce heat and simmer, stirring, for 10-15 minutes, or until potatoes are tender.

Remove from heat and blend until smooth. Return to saucepan and cook until heated through. Season with nutmeg and black pepper and serve.

Moroccan Lentil Soup

Serves 6-7

Ingredients:

1 cup red lentils

1 cup canned chickpeas, drained

1 onion, chopped

2 cloves garlic, minced

1 cup canned tomatoes, chopped

1 cup canned white beans, drained

3 carrots, diced

1 celery rib, diced

5 cups water

3 tbsp olive oil

1 tsp ginger, grated

1 tsp ground cardamom

1/2 tsp cumin

Directions:

In a large soup pot, sauté onions, garlic and ginger in olive oil for about 5 minutes. Add in water, lentils, chickpeas, white beans, tomatoes, carrots, celery, cardamom and cumin.

Bring to a boil for a few minutes then lower heat and simmer for half an hour or longer until the lentils are tender. Puree half the soup in a food processor or blender. Return the pureed soup to the pot, stir and serve.

Beetroot and Carrot Soup

Serves 5-6

Ingredients:

4 beets, washed and peeled

2 carrots, peeled, chopped

2 potatoes, peeled, chopped

1 small onion, chopped

2 cups vegetable broth

2 cups water

3 tbsp olive oil

1 cup finely cut green onions, to serve

Directions:

Heat olive oil in a deep saucepan over medium-high heat and sauté the onion and carrot until tender. Add in beets, potatoes, broth and water.

Bring to the boil then reduce heat and simmer, partially covered, for 30 minutes, or until beets are tender.

Set aside to cool then blend in batches until smooth. Return soup to saucepan and cook, stirring, for 4-5 minutes, or until heated through. Season with salt and pepper and serve sprinkled with green onions.

Celery, Apple and Carrot Soup

Serves 4

Ingredients:

2 celery ribs, chopped

1 large apple, chopped

1/2 small onion, chopped

3 carrots, chopped

2 garlic cloves, crushed

4 cups vegetable broth

3 tbsp olive oil

1 tsp ground ginger

salt and black pepper, to taste

Directions:

In a deep saucepan, heat olive oil over medium-high heat and sauté onion, garlic, celery and carrots for 3-4 minutes, stirring. Add in ginger, apple and vegetable broth.

Bring to a boil then reduce heat and simmer, covered, for 10 minutes. Blend until smooth and return to the pot. Cook over medium-high heat until heated through. Season with salt and pepper to taste and serve.

Pumpkin and Bell Pepper Soup

Serves 4

Ingredients:

1 medium leek, chopped

9 oz pumpkin, peeled, deseeded, cut into small cubes

1 red bell pepper, cut into small pieces

1 can tomatoes, undrained, crushed

3 cups vegetable broth

1/2 tsp cumin

salt and black pepper, to taste

Directions:

Heat the olive oil in a medium saucepan and sauté the leek for 4-5 minutes. Add in the pumpkin and bell pepper and cook, stirring, for 5 minutes. Add tomatoes, broth, and cumin and bring to a boil.

Cover, reduce heat to low, and simmer, stirring occasionally, for 30 minutes or until vegetables are soft. Season with salt and pepper and leave aside to cool. Blend in batches and reheat to serve.

Creamy Potato Soup

Serves 6-7

Ingredients:

4-5 medium potatoes, peeled and diced

2 carrots, chopped

1 zucchini, chopped

1 celery rib, chopped

5 cups water

3 tbsp olive oil

½ tsp dried rosemary

salt and black peppper, to taste

1/2 cup fresh parsley, finely cut

Directions:

In a deep soup pot, heat olive oil over medium heat and sauté the vegetables and rosemary for 2-3 minutes. Add in 4 cups of water and bring the soup to a boil then lower heat and simmer until all the vegetables are tender.

Blend soup in a blender until smooth. Serve warm, seasoned with black pepper and fresh parsley sprinkled over each serving.

Wild Mushroom Soup

Serves 4

Ingredients:

1 lb mixed wild mushrooms

1 onion, chopped

2 garlic cloves, crushed

1 tsp dried thyme

3 cups vegetable broth

3 tbsp olive oil

salt and pepper, to taste

Directions:

Sauté onions and garlic in a large soup pot untill transparent. Add thyme and mushrooms. Stir, and cook for 10 minutes, then add vegetable broth and simmer for another 10-20 minutes.

Blend, season and serve.

Spinach, Leek and Quinoa Soup

Serves 4-5

Ingredients:

½ cup quinoa, very well washed

2 leeks halved lengthwise and sliced

1 onion, chopped

2 garlic cloves, chopped

1 can diced tomatoes, (15 oz), undrained

2 cups fresh spinach, cut

4 cups vegetable broth

2 tbsp olive oil

salt and pepper, to taste

Directions:

Heat olive oil in a large soup pot over medium heat and sauté onion for 2 minutes, stirring. Add in leeks and cook for another 2-3 minutes. Stir in garlic, salt and black pepper to taste. Add the vegetable broth, canned tomatoes and quinoa.

Bring to a boil then reduce heat and simmer for 10 minutes. Stir in spinach and cook for another 5 minutes.

Vegetable Quinoa Soup

Serves 6

Ingredients:

½ cup quinoa

1/2 onion, chopped

1 potato, peeled and diced

1 carrot, diced

1 red bell pepper, chopped

2 tomatoes, chopped

1 small zucchini, peeled and diced

4 cups water

1 tsp dried oregano

3-4 tbsp olive oil

black pepper, to taste

2 tbsp fresh lemon juice

Directions:

Rinse quinoa very well in a fine mesh strainer under running water; set aside to drain.

Heat olive oil in a large soup pot and gently sauté the onion and carrot for 2-3 minutes, stirring every now and then. Add in potato, bell pepper, tomatoes, oregano and water.

Stir to combine, cover, and bring to a boil then lower heat and simmer for 10 minutes.

Add in quinoa and zucchini; cover and simmer for 15 minutes or until the vegetables are tender. Add in lemon juice; stir to combine and serve.

Slow Cooker Tuscan-style Soup

Serves 5-6

Ingredients:

1 lb potatoes, peeled and cubed

1 small onion, chopped

1 can mixed beans, drained

1 carrot, chopped

2 garlic cloves, chopped

4 cups chicken broth

1 cups chopped kale

3 tbsp olive oil

1 bay leaf

salt and pepper, to taste

Parmesan cheese, to serve

Directions:

Heat oil in a skillet over medium heat and sauté the onion, carrot and garlic, stirring, for 2-3 minutes or until soft.

Combine all ingredients except the kale into the slow cooker. Season with salt and pepper to taste.

Cook on high for 4 hours or low for 6-7 hours. Add in kale about 30 minutes before soup is finished cooking. Serve sprinkled with Parmesan cheese.

Lamb and Potato Casserole

Serves 6

Ingredients:

1 1/2 pounds shoulder lamb chops

12 small new potatoes, peeled, whole

3 onions, sliced

2 carrots, sliced

2 tbsp olive oil

2 tsp dried parsley

2 tsp dried mint

1/2 tsp pepper

1/2 tsp salt

Directions:

Place lamb chops into a greased casserole dish. Cover them with sliced onion, carrots, parsley, salt and pepper. Arrange new potatoes on and around the meat. Add enough cold water to fill the dish halfway and season with mint, salt and pepper.

Cover and bake, for 60 minutes, in a preheated to 350 F oven.

Mediterranean Baked Fish

Serves 4

Ingredients:

1 ½ flounder or sole fillets

3 tomatoes, chopped

1/2 onion, chopped

2 cloves garlic, chopped

1/3 cup white wine

20 black olives, pitted and chopped

1 tbsp capers

3 tbsp Parmesan cheese

3 tbsp olive oil

1 tbsp fresh lemon juice

1 tsp dried oregano

4 leaves fresh basil, chopped

Directions:

Heat olive oil in an ovenproof casserole dish and sauté onion until translucent, 2-3 minutes. Add in garlic, oregano, tomatoes, wine, olives, capers, lemon juice and the chopped basil.

Stir in Parmesan cheese and arrange fish in this sauce.

Bake for 30 minutes in a preheated to 350 F oven, until fish is easily flaked with a fork.

Mediterranean Chicken Casserole

Serves 4

Ingredients:

4-5 chicken breast halves

1 large onion, sliced

1 red bell pepper, thinly sliced

2 cups tomato pasta sauce

1/2 cup black olives, pitted

1/2 green olives, pitted

1/3 cup Parmesan cheese

1/2 cup chopped parsley

3 tbsp olive oil

salt and black pepper, to taste

Directions:

Heat olive oil in a large, deep saucepan over medium-high heat. Cook chicken breasts, turning, for 4 to 5 minutes or until golden.

Add in onion and bell pepper, pasta sauce and olives. Season with salt and pepper.

Cover, and simmer 30-35 minutes, stirring halfway through. Sprinkle with Parmesan cheese and parsley and serve.

Chicken and Potato Casserole

Serves 4

Ingredients:

4 skinless, boneless chicken breast halves

12 oz new potatoes

1 onion, sliced

2 carrots, cut

1 red bell pepper, halved, deseeded, cut

1 zucchini, peeled and cut

4 garlic cloves, thinly sliced

1 cup water

3 tbsp olive oil

1 tsp dried oregano

salt and pepper, to taste

Directions:

Heat olive oil in an ovenproof casserole dish and brown the chicken breasts.

Peel and cut all vegetables and add them on and around the chicken.

Season with salt and pepper, to taste. Sprinkle with oregano, add in water, and bake, uncovered, at 350 F for 45 minutes.

Mediterranean Chicken Drumstick Casserole

Serves 4

Ingredients:

8 chicken drumsticks

1 leek, trimmed, thinly sliced

2 garlic cloves, crushed

1 cup tomatoes, diced

1 cup black olives, pitted

1 cup canned chickpeas, drained and rinsed

2 tbsp olive oil

1 tsp dried rosemary

salt and black pepper, to taste

Directions:

Heat olive oil in an ovenproof casserole dish and brown the chicken drumsticks. Add in leek, garlic, tomatoes, chickpeas, olives and rosemary.

Cover, and bake in a preheated to 350 F oven, for 40 minutes, or until chicken is tender. Season with salt and pepper to taste.

Greek Chicken Casserole

Serves 5-6

Ingredients:

4-5 skinless, boneless chicken breast halves or 8 tights

2 lb potatoes, peeled and cubed

1/2 lb green beans, trimmed and cut in 1 inch pieces

1 large onion, chopped

2 cups diced, canned tomatoes, undrained

5 cloves garlic, minced

1/4 cup water

1 cup feta cheese, crumbled

salt and black pepper, to taste

Directions:

Heat olive oil in an ovenproof casserole dish and brown the chicken. Add in onion, thyme, black pepper and garlic, and sauté for a minute, stirring.

Add in potatoes, green beans, water and tomatoes, season with salt and pepper to taste, and top with crumbled feta. Cover and bake, in a preheated to 350 F oven, for 40 minutes.

Chicken with Almonds and Prunes

Serves 4

Ingredients:

1.5 lb chicken thigh fillets

1/3 cup fresh orange juice

2 tbsp honey

1/3 cup white wine

1/2 cup pitted prunes

2 tbsp blanched almonds

2 tbsp raisins or sultanas

1 tsp ground cinnamon

salt and black pepper, to taste

1/2 cup fresh parsley leaves, chopped, to serve

Directions:

Heat olive oil in a large saucepan over medium heat. Cook the chicken pieces until nicely browned, 3-4 minutes each side. Add in orange juice, wine, honey, prunes, almonds, raisins and cinnamon.

Bring to a boil, reduce heat to medium, and simmer 35 minutes, or until chicken is just tender. Season to taste with salt and pepper, sprinkle with parsley, and serve.

Chicken and Rice Casserole

Serves 6

Ingredients:

1 chicken 2-3 lbs, cut into serving pieces, or 2 lbs chicken thighs or breasts

1 medium onion, chopped

1 carrot, chopped

1 garlic clove, minced

1 1/2 cups white rice

2 cups chicken broth

2 cups water

1 cup of diced fresh or cooked tomatoes, drained

3 tbsp olive oil

1 tsp supper savory

1 tsp salt

black pepper, to taste

Directions:

Heat olive oil in an ovenproof casserole dish on medium-high heat. Cook chicken pieces for a few minutes on each side, enough to seal them.

Add in onions, garlic, carrot and rice and cook, stirring for 1-2 minutes, until the rice becomes transparent.

Stir in chicken broth, water and tomatoes, season with salt and pepper to taste, and bake in a preheated to 350 F oven for 45 minutes until the rice and chicken are done.

Easy Chicken Paella

Serves 4

Ingredients:

4 chicken thigh fillets, trimmed and cut into pieces

1 red onion, chopped

1 large red bell pepper, chopped

1 1/2 cups rice

2 cups chicken broth

1/2 cup frozen peas, thawed

1/2 cup parsley leaves, finely cut

1 tbsp paprika

1/2 tsp saffron

2 tbsp boiling water

2 tbsp olive oil

lemon wedges, to serve

Directions:

Place saffron in a small cup and add two tablespoons of boiling water. Set aside for 5 minutes.

Heat olive oil in a large saucepan over high heat and cook chicken 3-4 minutes or until golden. Add in onion and cook some more. Add paprika, red pepper and rice and stir to combine. Add saffron mixture, green peas and chicken broth then bring to a boil.

Reduce heat to low and simmer, covered, stirring from time to time, for 10-15 minutes, or until rice is just tender. Serve with lemon wedges.

Chicken and Artichoke Rice

Serves 4

Ingredients:

3 skinless chicken breasts, cut into strips

2 leeks, white parts only, chopped

7-8 canned artichoke hearts, quartered

2 garlic cloves, crushed

2/3 cup rice

2 cups chicken broth

2 tbsp olive oil

1 tsp lemon rind

7-8 fresh basil leaves, chopped

1 bay leaf

juice of 1 lemon

Directions:

Heat the oil in a large saucepan over low heat. Gently sauté the leeks, bay leaf and garlic for about 3-4 minutes, stirring occasionally. Add in the lemon rind and the chicken breasts and cook, stirring, for 5-6 minutes.

Add rice, stir, and add chicken broth and half the lemon juice.

Bring to the boil then reduce heat, cover, and cook for 10 minutes.

Set aside, covered, for 5 minutes then stir in the chopped basil, artichoke hearts and remaining lemon juice.

Easy Chicken Parmigiana

Serves 4

Ingredients:

4 chicken breast fillets

1 eggplant, peeled and sliced lengthwise

1 can tomatoes, diced

9 oz mozzarella cheese, sliced

2 tbsp olive oil

Directions:

In an ovenproof casserole, heat olive oil and brown the chicken pieces.

Place eggplant over the chicken and add in tomatoes. Top with mozzarella slices and bake in a preheated to 350 F for 20 minutes or until cheese is golden.

One-Pot Chicken Dijonnaise

Serves 4

Ingredients:

4 chicken breasts with skin

1 onion, sliced

5-6 white button mushrooms, sliced

2 garlic cloves, crushed

1 tbsp flour

1/3 cup Dijon mustard

1/3 cup mayonnaise

1/3 cup dry white wine

1/3 cup chicken broth

1/2 cup sour cream

2 tbsp olive oil

2 tbsp finely chopped tarragon

salt and pepper, to taste

Directions:

Heat oil in an ovenproof casserole over medium heat. Cook chicken in batches for 2-3 minutes each side until golden. Add onion and sauté for 3 more minutes or until soft. Stir in the mushrooms and garlic and cook, stirring, for a further minute. Add in flour and stir to combine. Add wine, mayonnaise, Dijon mustard, chicken broth and tarragon and combine well.

Cover with a lid or foil and bake in a preheated to 380 F oven for 10-15 minutes or until chicken is cooked through and the liquid has evaporated. Add in sour cream, salt and black pepper to taste and heat through.

Sweet and Sour Sicilian Chicken

Serves 4

Ingredients:

4 chicken thigh fillets

1 large red onion, sliced

3 garlic cloves, chopped

2 tbsp flour

1/3 cup dry white wine

1 cup chicken broth

1/2 cup green olives

2 tbsp olive oil

2 bay leaves

1 tbsp fresh oregano leaves

2 tbsp brown sugar or honey

2 tbsp red wine vinegar

salt and black pepper, to taste

Directions:

Combine the flour with salt and black pepper and coat well all chicken pieces. Heat oil in ovenproof casserole and cook the chicken in batches, for 1-2 minutes each side, or until golden.

Add in onion, garlic, and wine and cook, stirring for 1 more minute. Add the chicken broth, olives, bay leaves, oregano, sugar and vinegar and bake, in a preheated to 380 F oven, for 20 minutes, or until the chicken is cooked through.

Lemon Rosemary Chicken

Serves 4

Ingredients:

4 boneless skinless chicken breasts or 4-6 tights

2 garlic cloves, crushed

4-5 lemon slices

1 tbsp capers

1 tbsp dried rosemary

3 tbsp olive oil

salt and pepper, to taste

Directions:

Heat olive oil in a skillet over medium-low heat and sauté the garlic for about a minute.

Add the lemon slices to the bottom of the skillet and lay the chicken breasts on top of the lemon. Add in rosemary and capers, season with salt and pepper to taste, cover, and cook, on medium-low, for 20 minutes or until the chicken breasts are cooked through. Uncover and cook for 2-3 minutes, until the liquid evaporates.

Chicken and Bacon Frittata

Serves 4

Ingredients:

1/2 cup chicken, chopped finely

3 oz bacon, chopped

4-5 green onions, finely chopped

5 oz frozen chopped spinach, defrosted and excess moisture squeezed out

1 small tomato, diced

5 eggs whisked

4 tbsp milk

1/2 tsp dried thyme

4 tbsp olive oil

Directions:

Heat olive oil in an ovenproof pan and gently cook the chicken until almost cooked through. Add the green onions and tomato and cook for another minute. Add in the spinach and mix well.

In a medium bowl, whisk eggs, milk and thyme. Pour over the top of the meat and vegetable mixture, making sure it covers it well. Bake in a preheated to 360 F oven for about 15 minutes, or until eggs are cooked through.

Chicken and Zucchini Frittata

Serves 4

Ingredients:

1 cup chicken, chopped finely

3 green onions, finely chopped

1 garlic clove, chopped

1 zucchini, peeled and diced

1 tomato, diced

2 tbsp dill, finely chopped

5 eggs

1 cup grated Parmesan cheese

3 tbsp olive oil

In and ovenproof pan, heat olive oil and gently cook the chicken until almost cooked through. Add in the onion and garlic and cook for another minute, stirring.

Add the zucchini and tomato and cook for for 3-4 minutes, until lightly cooked.

In a medium bowl, whisk eggs, Parmesan cheese and dill together. Pour over the top of the chicken and vegetable mixture, making sure that it covers it well. Bake in a preheated to 360 F oven for around 15 minutes, until set. Garnish with fresh dill.

Beef and Pumpkin Stew

Serves 4-5

Ingredients:

2 lbs lean beef, cubed

2 cups cubed pumpkin

1 small onion, chopped

2 garlic cloves, chopped

1 tomato, diced

zest of one orange

1 bay leaf

1 tsp paprika

4 tbsp olive oil

salt and black pepper, to taste

3 green onions, chopped, to serve

Directions:

Heat a stew pot and brown the meat in olive oil.

Add remaining ingredients and sauté for 1-2 minutes.

Add enough water to cover everything, bring to a boil, reduce heat to low, cover, and simmer for 60 minutes, stirring occasionally, until beef is cooked through.

Sprinkle with green onions and serve.

Beef and Onion Stew

Serves 6

Ingredients:

2 lbs lean beef, cubed

3 lbs shallots, peeled

5 garlic cloves, peeled, whole

3 tbsp tomato paste

1 bay leaf

4 tbsp olive oil

3 tbsp red wine vinegar

1 tsp salt

Directions:

Heat a stew pot and brown the meat in olive oil.

Add in remaining ingredients and enough water to cover everything.

Bring to a boil, reduce heat to low, cover, and simmer for 90 minutes, stirring occasionally, until beef is cooked through.

Beef Stew with Green Peas

Serves 6

Ingredients:

2 lbs stewing beef

2 bags(10 oz each) frozen peas

1 onion, chopped

3-4 garlic cloves, cut

2 carrots, chopped

1/3 cup water

1/4 cup olive oil

1 tsp salt

1 tbsp paprika

1/2 cup fresh dill, finely chopped

1 cup yogurt (optional)

Directions:

Season the meat pieces with salt and black pepper. Heat olive oil in a large stewing pot and sauté onion and meat until the meat is well browned.

Add in paprika, carrots, garlic, frozen peas and water.

Bring to a boil, reduce heat, cover, and simmer for an hour. Serve sprinkled with fresh dill and a dollop of yogurt.

Beef and Spinach Stew

Serves 6

Ingredients:

1 lb stewing beef

10 oz frozen spinach or 6 cups fresh spinach leaves, chopped

1 onion, chopped

1 carrot, chopped

1 cup button white mushrooms, cut

1 tomato, diced

3 garlic cloves, crushed

1 cup beef broth

4 tbsp olive oil

6 oz butter

1 tbsp paprika

salt and pepper, to taste

Directions:

In a large stewing pot, heat the butter and olive oil and seal the beef pieces. Add in onion, carrot, mushrooms and garlic and sauté for a few minutes.

Add paprika and beef broth and bring to a boil then reduce heat and simmer, covered, for 40 minutes. Add in tomato and spinach, season with salt and pepper, stir, and simmer, uncovered, for 5 minutes more.

Mediterranean Beef Casserole

Serves 6

Ingredients:

2 lb lean steak, cut into large pieces

3 onions, sliced

4 garlic cloves, cut

2 red peppers, cut

1 green pepper, cut

1 zucchini, peeled and cut

3 tomatoes, quartered

2 tbsp tomato paste or purée

1/2 cup green olives, pitted

1/2 cup dry red wine

1/2 cup of water

1 tsp dried oregano

salt and black pepper, to taste

Directions:

Heat olive oil in a deep ovenproof casserole and seal the beef.

Add vegetables and stir to combine.

Dilute the tomato paste in half a cup of water and pour it over the meat mixture together with the wine.

Season with salt and pepper and bake, stirring halfway through, in a preheated to 350 F for one hour.

Beef and Broccoli Stir Fry

Serves 4

Ingredients:

1/2 lb flank steak, cut in strips

3 cups broccoli florets

1 onion, chopped

1 cup white button mushrooms, chopped

1 cup beef broth

1/3 cup cashew nuts

2 tbsp soy sauce

1 tbsp honey

1 tsp lemon zest

1 tsp grated ginger

3 tbsp olive oil

1 tsp cornstarch

Directions:

Place the meat in the freezer for 20 minutes then cut it in thin slices. Place it in a bowl together with soy sauce, honey, lemon zest and ginger. Stir to coat well and set aside for 30 minutes.

Stir fry steak in olive oil over high heat for 2-3 minutes until cooked through. Add and stir fry broccoli, onion, mushrooms and cashews. Stir in spice. Dilute cornstarch into beef broth and add it to the meat mixture. Stir until thickened.

Beef Stew with Quince

Serves 6-8

Ingredients:

2 lbs chuck roast, cut into 2 inch pieces

2 onions, chopped

2-3 tomatoes, pureed

1-2 bay leaves

1 cinnamon stick

1 cup dry white wine

3 quinces, peeled, cored and cubed

5-6 prunes

1 tsp paprika

1 tsp salt

1/2 tsp black pepper

1 tbsp honey

6 tbsp olive oil

Directions:

Heat olive oil in a large pot over medium-high heat. Seal the meat then add and sauté the onions for 6-8 minutes.

Add in the wine, bay leaves, cinnamon, tomato puree, salt, pepper, and enough water to cover the meat. Stir to combine and bring the pot to a simmer.

Add the quince to the stew pot along with the prunes and honey. Stir, cover, and simmer for two hours over low heat. Stir occasionally and make sure there is enough liquid in the pot. If it looks dry, add some water.

Before serving discard the bay leaves and the cinnamon stick.

Spanish Beef Stew

Serves 6-8

Ingredients:

2 lbs stewing beef

1 tbsp flour

1 cup beef broth

1/2 cup dry red wine

3 leeks, chopped

6 garlic cloves, halved

2 onions, chopped

1 carrot, sliced

1 celery rib, chopped

1 tomato, chopped

2 oz cooking chocolate

1/4 tsp cinnamon

1/4 cup olive oil

salt and pepper, to taste

Directions:

Heat the olive oil in a large pot. Seal the stewing meat for 3-4 minutes, or until well browned on all sides. Add in the flour and stir. Add the wine and cook for 2-3 minutes, stirring. Add the garlic, onions, tomatoes, carrot, celery and leaks to the pot and stir to combine. Add chocolate and beef broth, stir, and bring to a boil.

Reduce heat, cover partially and simmer for an hour and a half or until the meat is cooked through.

Ground Beef and Chickpea Casserole

Serves 6

Ingredients:

1 lb ground beef

1 onion, chopped

2 garlic cloves, crushed

1 can chickpeas, drained

1 can sweet corn, drained

1 can tomato sauce

1/2 cup water

2 bay leaves

1 tsp dried oregano

1/2 tsp salt

1/2 tsp cumin

3 tbsp olive oil

black pepper, to taste

Directions:

Heat olive oil in a casserole over medium-high heat. Add in the onion and sauté for 4-5 minutes. Add garlic and sauté for 1-2 minutes more. Add in the ground beef and cook for 5 minutes, stirring, until browned. Stir in cumin and bay leaves, tomatoes, corn and chickpeas.

Bake in a preheated to 350 F for 20 minutes, or until the beef is cooked through. Remove the bay leaves and serve over rice pilaf or couscous.

Spinach with Ground Beef

Serves 4

Ingredients:

10 oz ground beef

6 cups fresh spinach, chopped

1 tomato, cubed

1 onion, finely chopped

1/3 cup rice

4 tbsp olive oil

1 tsp paprika

salt, to taste

black pepper, to taste

Directions:

Heat olive oil in a large pot and sauté the onion for about 2-3 minutes. Add in ground beef, paprika, salt and black pepper and stir to combine.

Cook until the ground beef turns brown. Stir in rice, the diced tomato and simmer, covered, for 20 minutes.

Add spinach and cook until it wilts. Serve with a dollop of yogurt.

Delicious One-Pot Ground Beef Pasta

Serves 4

Ingredients:

8 oz dry pasta

1 lb ground beef

3 cups hot water

1/2 onion, finely cut

4-5 white button mushrooms, chopped

2 garlic cloves, chopped

6-7 gherkins, finely chopped

1/2 cup sweet corn

1 cup parsley, finely cut

1/2 cup heavy cream

3 tbsp olive oil

salt and black pepper, to taste

Directions:

Heat olive oil in deep saucepan and sauté the onion for about 2-3 minutes. Add in ground beef and sauté for 3-4 minutes or until the beef turns brown. Add in hot water, pasta, mushrooms, garlic, gherkins, sweet corn and parsley and simmer for 10 minutes.

Add in the cream, salt and peppper to taste and Parmesan cheese. Stir and simmer for 1-2 minutes more. Remove from heat and set aside for a few minutes. Taste to adjust seasonings and serve.

Sausage and Beans

Serves 4

Ingredients:

1.7 lb lean beef sausages

1 big onion, thinly sliced

2 garlic cloves, crushed

2 cups canned white beans, drained, rinsed

1 cup canned tomatoes, drained, diced

1 tsp paprika

1 tbsp dried mint

1 tbsp sunflower oil

1/2 cup finely cut parsley, to serve

Directions:

Heat a large non-stick frying pan over medium heat. Cook sausages for 8 to 10 minutes or until browned.

Add in onions, garlic and paprika and sauté gently for 3-4 minutes or until onion is soft. Add beans, tomatoes and mint. Stir, and simmer for 15 minutes or until sauce is thick. Serve into bowls sprinkled with fresh parsley.

Mediterranean Pork Casserole

Serves 4

Ingredients:

1 1/2 lb pork loin, cut into cubes

1 large onion, chopped

1 cup white button mushrooms, cut

2 garlic cloves, finely chopped

1 green pepper, deseeded and cut into strips

1 red pepper, deseeded and cut into strips

2 tomatoes, chopped

½ cup chicken broth

2 tbsp olive oil

1 tsp summer savory

1 tsp paprika

salt and black pepper, to taste

Directions:

Add the olive oil to a casserole dish and seal the pork cubes for about 5 minutes, stirring continuously. Lower the heat, add the onion and garlic and sauté for 3-4 minutes until the onion is soft.

Stir in paprika and savory and season with salt and black pepper to taste. Add in peppers, tomatoes, chicken broth and mushrooms. Cover with a lid or aluminum foil and bake for 1 hour at 350 F, or until the pork is tender. Uncover and bake for 5 minutes more. Serve with mashed potatoes or rice pilaf.

Pork and Rice Casserole

Serves 5-6

Ingredients:

1.5 lb pork, cubed (leg or neck)

1 onion, chopped

2 cups rice, washed

5 cups water

4 tbsp olive oil

1/2 cup finely cut parsley leaves, to serve

Directions:

Heat oil in a large ovenproof casserole dish on medium-high heat. Cook pork, turning, for 4-5 minutes, or until browned.

Add rice and cook for 2-3 minutes, stirring continuously, until transparent. Add 5 cups of warm water, stir well, and bake in a preheated to 350 F oven for 40 minutes, stirring halfway through.

When ready, sprinkle with parsley, set aside for 2-3 minutes and serve.

Pork Roast and Cabbage

Serves 4

Ingredients:

2 cups cooked pork roast, chopped

1/2 head cabbage

1 onion, chopped

1 lemon, juice only

1 tomato, chopped

2 tbsp olive oil

1 tsp paprika

1/2 tsp cumin

black pepper, to taste

Directions:

In an ovenproof casserole dish, heat olive oil and gently sauté cabbage, pork and onions. Add in cumin, paprika, lemon juice, tomato and stir.

Cover and bake at 350 F for 20-25 minutes, or until vegetables are tender.

Orange Pork Chops

Serves 4

Ingredients:

4 pork chops, about 4 oz each

1 onion, thinly sliced

4 garlic cloves, crushed

3 tbsp olive oil

1/4 tsp cumin

1/2 tsp dried oregano

1 tsp black pepper

1 tbsp raw honey

1 cup orange juice

Directions:

Crush the garlic, oregano, black pepper and cumin together into a paste. Rub each chop with the garlic paste and arrange them in a casserole dish.

Dilute one tablespoon of honey into the orange juice and pour it over the chops. Add in onions, stir, and bake in a preheated to 350 F on for 30 minutes, or until the chops are cooked through.

Pork and Mushroom Crock Pot

Serves 4

Ingredients:

2 lbs pork tenderloin, sliced

2 cups chopped white button mushrooms

1 can cream of mushroom soup

½ cup sour cream

4 tbsp chopped taragon

1/2 tsp black pepper

1/2 tsp salt

Directions:

Spray the slow cooker with non stick spray.

Combine all ingredients into the slow cooker. Cover, and cook on low for 7-9 hours.

Bacon and Mushroom Frittata

Serves 4

Ingredients:

6-7 oz bacon, chopped

1 cup white button mushrooms, chopped

½ onion, chopped

1 garlic clove, chopped

1 tomato, thinly sliced

1/2 tsp black pepper

1 tsp dried parsley

5 eggs, whisked

3 tbsp milk

1 tbsp olive oil

Directions:

In and ovenproof pan, heat olive oil and gently cook the bacon until almost cooked through. Add in the onion and garlic and cook for another minute, stirring. Add the mushrooms, stir, and cook on medium-high heat for 3-4 minutes.

In a medium bowl, whisk eggs, milk, salt, black pepper and parsley together. Pour over the top of the bacon and mushroom mixture, making sure that it covers it well. Lay the tomato slices on top and bake in a preheated to 360 F oven for around 15 minutes, until set.

Brussels Sprouts with Bacon and Onion

Serves 6

Ingredients:

4 strips bacon, cut

2 tbsp olive oil

2 lb Brussels sprouts, halved

1 large onion, chopped

1/2 cup sour cream

salt and freshly ground black pepper, to taste

Directions:

In an ovenproof casserole, cook bacon over medium-high heat until crispy.

Add in onions and Brussels sprouts and bake, in a preheated to 350 F oven, stirring occasionally, until sprouts are golden brown. Stir in sour cream, sprinkle with Parmesan cheese and bake for 5 more minutes.

Zucchini Bake

Serves 4

Ingredients:

5 medium zucchinis, peeled and grated

1 carrot, grated

1 small tomato, diced

1 onion, halved, thinly sliced

2 garlic cloves, crushed

1 cup self-raising flour, sifted

5 eggs, lightly whisked

1/3 cup sunflower oil

1/2 cup fresh dill, finely cut

1 cup grated feta cheese

2 cups yogurt, to serve (optional)

Directions:

Combine zucchinis, carrot, tomato, onion, garlic, and dill in a bowl. Add flour, eggs, oil and cheese. Season and stir to combine.

Transfer the zucchini mixture into a greased casserole dish and bake for 20-30 minutes in a preheated to 350 F oven. Serve with yogurt.

Baked Cauliflower

Serves 4

Ingredients:

1 medium cauliflower, cut into florets

4 garlic cloves, lightly crushed

4-5 fresh rosemary leaves, finely cut

salt, to taste

black pepper, to taste

1/4 cup olive oil

1/2 cup sour cream

1/2 cup grated Parmesan Cheese

Directions:

In a bowl, mix oil, rosemary, salt, pepper and garlic together. Add in cauliflower florets and toss to combine.

Place in a casserole dish in one layer. Roast in a preheated oven at 350 F for 20 minutes.

Stir in sour cream, sprinkle with Parmesan cheese and bake for 10 more minutes.

Potato and Zucchini Bake

Serves 6

Ingredients:

1½ lb potatoes, peeled and sliced into rounds

5 zucchinis, peeled and sliced into rounds

2 onions, sliced

3 tomatoes, pureed

½ cup water

4 tbsp olive oil

1 tsp dried oregano

1/3 cup fresh parsley leaves, chopped

salt and black pepper, to taste

Directions:

Place potatoes, zucchinis and onions in a large, shallow ovenproof baking dish. Pour over the olive oil and pureed tomatoes. Add salt and freshly ground pepper to taste and toss the everything together. Add in water.

Bake in a preheated to 350 F oven for 45 minutes, stirring halfway through.

Artichoke and Onion Frittata

Serves 4

Ingredients:

1 small onion, chopped

1 cup marinated artichoke hearts, drained

6 eggs

1 garlic clove, crushed

1 tbsp olive oil

salt and freshly ground black pepper

1/2 cup fresh parsley, finely cut, to serve

Directions:

Heat oil in a non-stick oven pan over medium heat and sauté onion stirring occasionally, for 5-6 minutes or until golden brown. Add artichokes and cook for 2 minutes or until heated through.

Whisk eggs with garlic until combined well. Season with salt and pepper. Pour the egg mixture over the artichoke mixture.

Reduce heat, cover, and cook for 10 minutes or until the frittata is set around the edge but still runny in the center. Place pan into preheated oven and cook 4-5 until golden brown.

Remove from oven and cut into wedges. Serve sprinkled with parsley.

Green Pea and Mushroom Stew

Serves 4

Ingredients:

1 cup green peas (fresh or frozen)

5 large white button mushrooms, sliced

3 green onions, chopped

1 big carrot, chopped

1-2 cloves garlic

4 tbsp sunflower oil

1/2 cup water

1/2 cup finely chopped dill

salt and black pepper, to taste

Directions:

In a saucepan, sauté mushrooms, carrot, green onions and garlic. Add in green peas and simmer for 10 minutes until tender.

When ready, sprinkle with dill, and serve.

Tomato and Leek Stew

Serves 5-6

Ingredients:

1 lb leeks, cut into rings

1/2 cup vegetable broth

2 tbsp tomato paste

4 tbsp sunflower oil

1 tbsp dried mint

salt to taste

fresh ground pepper to taste

Directions:

Heat oil in a heavy wide saucepan or sauté pan. Add in leeks, salt, pepper, and sauté, stirring, for 5 minutes.

Add in vegetable broth and bring to a boil.

Cover, and simmer over low heat, stirring often, for about 10-15 minutes or until leeks are tender. Gently stir in tomato paste and dried mint, raise heat to medium, uncover, and simmer for 5 more minutes.

Potato and Leek Stew

Serves 4

Ingredients:

12 oz potatoes, diced

2-3 leeks cut into thick rings

5-6 tbsp olive oil

1 cup water

1/2 cup finely cut parsley

1 tsp paprika

salt and black pepper, to taste

Directions:

Heat olive oil in a heavy wide saucepan or sauté pan. Add in leeks, paprika, salt and pepper, and sauté for 2-3 minutes, stirring.

Add in potatoes and water. The water should cover the vegetables. Bring to a boil and simmer until vegetables are tender. Sprinkle with finely chopped parsley and serve.

Baked Beans and Rice Casserole

Serves 4

Ingredients

1 15 oz can white or red beans, drained

1/2 cup rice

1 cup water

1 onion, chopped

½ bunch parsley, finely cut

1 tbsp dried mint

3 tbsp olive oil

1 tbsp paprika

½ tsp black pepper

1 tsp salt

Directions:

Heat olive oil in a deep ovenproof casserole and gently sauté the chopped onion. Add in paprika and rice and cook, stirring, for a minute.

Add in water or vegetable broth and beans. Season with salt and black pepper, stir in mint and parsley, and bake in a preheated to 350 F oven for 20 minutes.

Creamy Green Pea and Rice Casserole

Serves 4

Ingredients

1 onion, very finely cut

1 bag frozen peas

2-3 garlic cloves, chopped

3-4 mushrooms, chopped

1/2 cup white rice

1 cup water

4 tbsp olive oil

1/2 cup sour cream

2/3 cup grated Parmesan cheese

1/2 cup fresh dill, finely cut

salt and black pepper, to taste

Directions:

In a deep ovenproof casserole dish, heat olive oil and sauté the onions, garlic and mushrooms for 2-3 minutes. Add in rice and cook, stirring, for 1 minute. Add in a cup of warm water, the frozen peas, and the dill.

Stir to combine and bake in a preheated to 350 F oven, for 20 minutes.

Stir in sour cream, sprinkle with Parmesan cheese, bake for 2-3 more minutes, and serve.

Zucchini and Rice Stew

Serves 4

Ingredients:

2 lbs zucchinis, diced

1 cup green onions, finely chopped

5 tbsp sunflower oil

2 cups water

2 tomatoes, diced

1 tsp salt

1 tsp paprika

salt and black pepper, to taste

2½ cups water

1 cup chopped fresh dill

Directions:

Gently sauté green onions in oil and a little water.

Transfer onions in a baking dish, add in zucchinis, tomatoes, rice, salt, paprika, pepper and water.

Stir to combine, cover with a lid or foil and bake in preheated to 350 F oven for 30 minutes, or until rice is done. Sprinkle with dill.

Spinach with Rice

Serves 4

Ingredients:

1.5 lb fresh spinach, washed, drained and chopped

1/2 cup rice

1 onion, chopped

1 carrot, chopped

5 tbsp olive oil

2 cups water

Directions:

Heat oil in a large skillet and cook the onions and the carrot until soft. Add in paprika and rice and stir.

Add two cups of warm water stirring constantly as the rice absorbs it, and simmer for 10 minutes.

Wash the spinach cut it in strips then add to the rice and cook until it wilts. Remove from heat and season to taste.

Eggplant Casserole

Serves 4

Ingredients:

2 medium eggplants, peeled and diced

1 cup canned tomatoes, drained and diced

1 zucchini, peeled and diced

9-10 black olives, pitted

1 onion, chopped

4 garlic cloves, chopped

2 tbsp tomato paste

1 cup canned tomatoes, drained and diced

3 tbsp olive oil

1 tbsp paprika

salt and black pepper, to taste

1 cup parsley, chopped, to serve

Directions:

Heat olive oil in a deep casserole dish and gently sauté onions, garlic, and eggplants. Add in paprika and tomato paste and sauté, stirring, for 1-2 minutes. Add in the rest of the ingredients.

Cover, and bake at 350 F for 30-40 minutes. Sprinkle with parsley and serve.

Eggplant and Chickpea Casserole

Serves 4

Ingredients:

2-3 eggplants, peeled and diced

1 onion, chopped

2-3 garlic cloves, crushed

1 can chickpeas, (15 oz), drained

1 can tomatoes, (15 oz), undrained, diced

1 tsp paprika

½ tsp cinnamon

1 tsp cumin

4 tbsp olive oil

salt and pepper, to taste

1 cup grated Parmesan cheese

Directions:

Peel and dice the eggplants. Heat olive oil in a deep ovenproof casserole and sauté the onions and crushed garlic.

Add in paprika, cumin and cinnamon. Stir well to coat evenly. Sauté for 3-4 minutes until the onions have softened.

Add the eggplant, tomatoes and chickpeas. Bake in a preheated to 350 F oven, covered, for 15 minutes, or until the eggplant is tender.

Uncover and sprinkle with Parmesan cheese. Bake for a few more minutes until the liquid evaporates and the cheese is golden.

Ratatouille

Serves 4

Ingredients:

1 eggplant, cut into small cubes

2 large tomatoes, chopped

2 zucchinis, sliced

1 onion, sliced into rings

1 green pepper, sliced

6-7 sliced white button mushrooms

3 cloves garlic, crushed

2 tsp dried parsley

½ cup Parmesan cheese

3 tbsp olive oil

Directions:

Place eggplant pieces on a tray and sprinkle with plenty of salt. Let sit for 30 minutes, then rinse with cold water.

Heat olive oil in an ovenproof casserole over medium heat. Gently sauté garlic for a minute or two. Add in parsley and eggplant. Continue sautéing until eggplant is soft. Sprinkle with a tablespoon of Parmesan cheese. Spread zucchinis in an even layer over the eggplant. Sprinkle with a little more cheese. Continue layering onion, mushrooms, pepper and tomatoes, covering each layer with a sprinkling of Parmesan cheese. Bake in a preheated to 350 F oven for 40 minutes.

Rice Stuffed Bell Peppers

Serves 4-5

Ingredients:

8 bell peppers, cored and seeded

1 1/2 cups rice

2 onions, chopped

1 tomato, chopped

1/2 cup fresh parsley, chopped

3 tbsp olive oil

1 tbsp paprika

Directions:

Heat the olive oil and sauté the onions for 2-3 minutes. Add in paprika, rice, diced tomato and season with salt and pepper. Add ½ cup of hot water and cook the rice, stirring, until the water is absorbed.

Stuff each pepper with rice mixture using a spoon. Every pepper should be ¾ full. Arrange the peppers in a deep ovenproof dish and top up with warm water to half fill the dish.

Cover and bake for about 20 minutes at 350 F. Uncover and cook for another 15 minutes until the peppers are well cooked through.

Green Bean and Potato Stew

Serves 5-6

Ingredients:

2 cups green beans, fresh or frozen

2 onions, chopped

3-4 potatoes, peeled and diced

2 carrots, cut

4 cloves garlic, crushed

1 cup fresh parsley, chopped

1/2 cup fresh dill, finely chopped

4 tbsp olive oil

1/2 cup water

2 tsp tomato paste

salt and pepper, to taste

Directions:

Heat olive oil in a deep saucepan and gently sauté the onions and garlic. Add in green beans and the remaining ingredients.

Cover and simmer over medium heat for about an hour or until all vegetables are tender.

Check after 30 minutes; add more water if necessary. Serve sprinkled with fresh dill.

Cabbage and Rice Stew

Serves 4

Ingredients:

1 cup long grain white rice

2 cups water

2 tbsp olive oil

1 small onion, chopped

1 clove garlic, crushed

1/4 head cabbage, cored and shredded

2 tomatoes, diced

1 tbsp paprika

1/2 cup parsley, finely cut

salt and black peppper, to taste

Directions:

Heat the olive oil in a large pot. Add in onion and garlic and cook until transparent. Add paprika, rice and water, stir, and bring to boil.

Simmer for 10 minutes. Add in cabbage, tomatoes, and cook for about 20 minutes, stirring occasionally, until the cabbage cooks down. Season with salt and pepper and serve sprinkled with parsley.

Rice with Leeks and Olives

Serves 4-6

Ingredients:

6 large leeks, cleaned and sliced into bite sized pieces (about 6-7 cups of sliced leeks)

1 large onion, cut

20 black olives pitted, chopped

1/2 cup hot water

1/4 cup olive oil

1 cup rice

2 cups boiling water

black pepper, to taste

Directions:

In a large saucepan, sauté the leeks and onion in olive oil for 4-5 minutes. Cut and add the olives and 1/2 cup of water. Bring temperature down, cover saucepan, and cook for 5 minutes, stirring occasionally.

Add in rice and 2 cups of hot water, bring to a boil, cover, and simmer for 15 more minutes, stirring occasionally.

Remove from heat and allow to 'sit' for 30 minutes before serving so that the rice can absorb any liquid left.

Rice and Tomato Stew

Serves 6-7

Ingredients:

1 cup rice

1 big onion, chopped

2 cups canned tomatoes, diced or 5 big ripe tomatoes

1 tbsp paprika

1/4 cup olive oil

1 tsp summer savory

½ cup fresh parsley, finely cut

1 tsp sugar

Directions:

Wash and drain the rice. In a large saucepan, sauté the onion in olive oil for 4-5 minutes. Add in paprika and rice, stirring constantly, until the rice becomes transparent.

Stir in 2 cups of hot water and the tomatoes. Mix well and season with salt, pepper, savory and a tsp of sugar to neutralize the acidic taste of the tomatoes. Simmer over medium heath for about 20 minutes. When ready sprinkle with parsley.

Okra and Tomato Casserole

Serves 4-5

Ingredients:

1 lb okra, stem ends trimmed

4 large tomatoes, cut into wedges

3 garlic cloves, chopped

3 tbsp olive oil

1 tsp salt

black pepper, to taste

Directions:

In a large casserole, mix together trimmed okra, sliced tomatoes, olive oil and chopped garlic. Add salt and pepper and toss to combine.

Bake in a preheated to 350 F oven for 45 minutes, or until the okra is tender.

Spinach with Eggs

Serves 2

Ingredients:

1 lb spinach, fresh or frozen

1 onion, finely cut

4 eggs

3 tbsp olive oil

1/4 tsp cumin

1 tsp paprika

salt and pepper, to taste

Heat olive oil on medium-low heat in a skillet. Gently sauté onion for 3-4 minutes. Add paprika and cumin and stir to combine.

Add spinach and sauté some more until it wilts. Season with salt and black pepper to taste.

Prepare 4 holes on the spinach bed for the eggs. Break an egg into each hole.

Cover and cook until eggs are cooked through. Serve with bread and a dollop of yogurt.

Mish-Mash

Serves 5-6

Ingredients:

1 onion, chopped

1 green bell pepper, chopped

1 red bell peppers chopped

4 tomatoes, cubed

8-9 eggs

9 oz feta cheese, crumbled

3 tbsp olive oil

1/2 cup parsley, finely cut

salt and black pepper, to taste

Directions:

In a large pan sauté onions over medium heat, till transparent. Reduce heat and add bell peppers and garlic. Continue cooking until soft. Add the tomatoes and continue simmering until the mixture is almost dry.

Add the cheese and all eggs and cook until well mixed and not too liquid. Season with black pepper and remove from heat. Sprinkle with parsley and serve.

Vegetable Quinoa Pilaf

Serves 6

Ingredients:

1 cup quinoa

2 cups water

1 red bell pepper, chopped

1 small eggplant, chopped

1 zucchini, chopped

1/2 onion, thinly sliced

2 garlic cloves, cut

1 tsp summer savory

1 tsp dried oregano

3 tbsp olive oil

salt and pepper, to taste

Directions:

Rinse quinoa very well in a fine mesh strainer under running water; set aside to drain.

Heat olive oil in a heavy based saucepan over medium-high heat. Add the bell pepper, eggplant, onion, garlic and zucchini. Sauté, stirring, for 2 minutes then add in the spice, salt and black peppper, water and quinoa and bring to a boil. Lower heat, cover, and simmer for 15 minutes.

Spinach, Lentil and Quinoa Casserole

Serves 6

Ingredients:

½ cup brown lentils

½ cup quinoa

3 cups fresh spinach or about half package of frozen spinach, thawed

1 onion, chopped

2 medium carrots, chopped

2 cloves garlic, cut

3 tbsp olive oil

1 tbsp paprika

2 tsp summer savory

2 cups water

salt and black pepper, to taste

Directions:

Heath the olive oil in a deep casserole dish and gently sauté the onion and carrots for 4-5 minutes. Add in garlic, paprika, savory and lentils and sauté for a minute more while stirring. Stir in the water and bake at 350 F for 15 minutes.

Wash and rinse the quinoa and add it to the casserole with salt and pepper to taste. Stir well and bake for another 10 minutes. Cut the spinach and add it to casserole dish. Bake for 4-5 more minutes and serve.

Rich Vegetable One-Pot Pasta

Serves 4

Ingredients:

12 oz dry pasta

11/2 cup tomato sauce

2 cups water

1/2 onion, finely chopped

1 cup white button mushrooms, chopped

1/3 cup black olives, pitted

1/2 small eggplant, peeled and cubed

1 red pepper, cut

3 tbsp olive oil

1 tsp dried basil

1 tsp black pepper

1 tsp salt

1/2 cup parsley, finely cut

Directions:

In a large saucepan, heat olive oil over medium-high heat. Gently sauté the finely chopped onion and red pepper for 1-2 minutes. Add in the mushrooms and eggplant and sauté for a few minutes more, stirring.

Add the tomato sauce, water, salt, peppper, basil and black olives and bring to a boil. Add in pasta, cover, and simmer for about 10 minutes or until the pasta is cooked to al dente. Taste to adjust seasonings, sprinkle with parsley and serve.

One-Pot Broccoli Pasta

Serves 4

Ingredients:

8 oz dry pasta

1.5 lb broccoli, cut into florets

4 cups water

1/2 onion, finely chopped

4-5 white button mushrooms, chopped

2 garlic cloves, chopped

1/2 cup frozen peas

1/2 cup sweet corn

1/4 cup heavy cream

3 tbsp olive oil

1 tsp dried basil

salt and black pepper, to taste

a handful of baby rocket leaves, to serve

Directions:

Add water, pasta, broccoli, mushrooms, garlic, onion, peas and sweet corn to a large pot, set over high heat, and bring to a boil. Lower heat and simmer for 10 minutes, stirring constantly.

Add in the cream, salt and peppper to taste and simmer for 1-2 minutes more. Remove from heat and set aside for a few minutes. Taste to adjust seasonings, sprinkle with baby rocket leaves, and serve.

FREE BONUS RECIPES: 10 Ridiculously Easy Jam and Jelly Recipes Anyone Can Make

A Different Strawberry Jam

Makes 6-7 11 oz jars

Ingredients:

4 lb fresh small strawberries (stemmed and cleaned)

5 cups sugar

1 cup water

2 tbsp lemon juice or 1 tsp citric acid

Directions:

Mix water and sugar and bring to the boil. Simmer sugar syrup for 5-6 minutes then slowly drop in the cleaned strawberries. Stir and bring to the boil again. Lower heat and simmer, stirring and skimming any foam off the top once or twice. Drop a small amount of the jam on a plate and wait a minute to see if it has thickened. If it has gelled enough, turn off the heat. If not, keep boiling and test every 5 minutes until ready. Two or three minutes before you remove the jam from the heat, add lemon juice or citric acid and stir well.

Ladle the hot jam in the jars until 1/8-inch from the top. Place the lid on top and flip the jar upside down. Continue until all of the jars are filled and upside down. Allow the jam to cool completely before turning right-side up. Press on the lid to check and see if it has sealed. If one of the jars lids doesn't pop up- the jar is not sealed- store it in a refrigerator.

Raspberry Jam

Makes 4-5 11 oz jars

Ingredients:

4 cups raspberries

4 cups sugar

1 tsp vanilla extract

1/2 tsp citric acid

Directions:

Gently wash and drain the raspberries. Lightly crush them with a potato masher, food mill or a food processor. Do not puree, it is better to have bits of fruit. Sieve half of the raspberry pulp to remove some of the seeds. Combine sugar and raspberries in a wide, thick-bottomed pot and bring mixture to a full rolling boil, stirring constantly. Skim any scum or foam that rises to the surface. Boil until the jam sets.

Test by putting a small drop on a cold plate – if the jam is set, it will wrinkle when given a small poke with your finger. Add citric acid, vanilla, and stir. Simmer for 2-3 minutes more, then ladle into hot jars. Flip upside down or process 10 minutes in boiling water.

Raspberry-Peach Jam

Makes 4-5 11 oz jars

Ingredients:

2 lb peaches

1 1/2 cup raspberries

4 cups sugar

1 tsp citric acid

Directions:

Wash and slice the peaches. Clean the raspberries and combine them with the peaches is a wide, heavy-bottomed saucepan. Cover with sugar and set aside for a few hours or overnight. Bring the fruit and sugar to a boil over medium heat, stirring occasionally. Remove any foam that rises to the surface.

Boil until the jam sets. Add citric acid and stir. Simmer for 2-3 minutes more, then ladle into hot jars. Flip upside down or process 10 minutes in boiling water.

Blueberry Jam

Makes 4-5 11 oz jars

Ingredients:

4 cups granulated sugar

3 cups blueberries (frozen and thawed or fresh)

3/4 cup honey

2 tbsp lemon juice

1 tsp lemon zest

Directions:

Gently wash and drain the blueberries. Lightly crush them with a potato masher, food mill or a food processor. Add the honey, lemon juice, and lemon zest, then bring to a boil over medium-high heat. Boils for 10-15 minutes, stirring from time to time. Boil until the jam sets.

Test by putting a small drop on a cold plate – if the jam is set, it will wrinkle when given a small poke with your finger. Skim off any foam, then ladle the jam into jars. Seal, flip upside down or process for 10 minutes in boiling water.

Triple Berry Jam

Makes 4-5 11 oz jars

Ingredients:

1 cup strawberries

1 cup raspberries

2 cups blueberries

4 cups sugar

1 tsp citric acid

Directions:

Mix berries and add sugar. Set aside for a few hours or overnight. Bring the fruit and sugar to the boil over medium heat, stirring frequently. Remove any foam that rises to the surface. Boil until the jam sets. Add citric acid, salt and stir.

Simmer for 2-3 minutes more, then ladle into hot jars. Flip upside down or process 10 minutes in boiling water.

Red Currant Jelly

Makes 6-7 11 oz jars

Ingredients:

2 lb fresh red currants

1/2 cup water

3 cups sugar

1 tsp citric acid

Directions:

Place the currants into a large pot, and crush with a potato masher or berry crusher. Add in water, and bring to a boil. Simmer for 10 minutes. Strain the fruit through a jelly or cheese cloth and measure out 4 cups of the juice. Pour the juice into a large saucepan, and stir in the sugar. Bring to full rolling boil, then simmer for 20-30 minutes, removing any foam that may rise to the surface. When the jelly sets, ladle in hot jars, flip upside down or process in boiling water for 10 minutes.

White Cherry Jam

Makes 3-4 11 oz jars

Ingredients:

2 lb cherries

3 cups sugar

2 cups water

1 tsp citric acid

Directions:

Wash and stone cherries. Combine water and sugar and bring to the boil. Boil for 5-6 minutes then remove from heat and add cherries. Bring to a rolling boil and cook until set. Add citric acid, stir and boil 1-2 minutes more.

Ladle in hot jars, flip upside down or process in boiling water for 10 minutes.

Cherry Jam

Makes 3-4 11 oz jars

Ingredients:

2 lb fresh cherries, pitted, halved

4 cups sugar

1/2 cup lemon juice

Directions:

Place the cherries in a large saucepan. Add sugar and set aside for an hour. Add the lemon juice and place over low heat. Cook, stirring occasionally, for 10 minutes or until sugar dissolves. Increase heat to high and bring to a rolling boil.

Cook for 5-6 minutes or until jam is set. Remove from heat and ladle hot jam into jars, seal and flip upside down.

Oven Baked Ripe Figs Jam

Makes 3-4 11 oz jars

Ingredients:

2 lb ripe figs

2 cups sugar

1 ½ cups water

2 tbsp lemon juice

Directions:

Arrange the figs in a Dutch oven, if they are very big, cut them in halves. Add sugar and water and stir well. Bake at 350 F for about one and a half hours. Do not stir. You can check the readiness by dropping a drop of the syrup in a cup of cold water – if it falls to the bottom without dissolving, the jam is ready. If the drop dissolves before falling, you can bake it a little longer. Take out of the oven, add lemon juice and ladle in the warm jars. Place the lids on top and flip the jars upside down. Allow the jam to cool completely before turning right-side up.

If you want to process the jams - place them into a large pot, cover the jars with water by at least 2 inches and bring to a boil. Boil for 10 minutes, remove the jars and sit to cool.

Quince Jam

Makes 5-6 11 oz jars

Ingredients:

4 lb quinces

5 cups sugar

2 cups water

1 tsp lemon zest

3 tbsp lemon juice

Directions:

Combine water and sugar in a deep, thick-bottomed saucepan and bring it to the boil. Simmer, stirring until the sugar has completely dissolved. Rinse the quinces, cut in half, and discard the cores. Grate the quinces, using a cheese grater or a blender to make it faster. Quince flesh tends to darken very quickly, so it is good to do this as fast as possible. Add the grated quinces to the sugar syrup and cook uncovered, stirring occasionally until the jam turns pink and thickens to desired consistency, about 40 minutes. Drop a small amount of the jam on a plate and wait a minute to see if it has thickened. If it has gelled enough, turn off the heat. If not, keep boiling and test every 2-3 minutes until ready. Two or three minutes before you remove the jam from the heat, add lemon juice and lemon zest and stir well.

Ladle in hot, sterilized jars and flip upside down.

Printed in Dunstable, United Kingdom